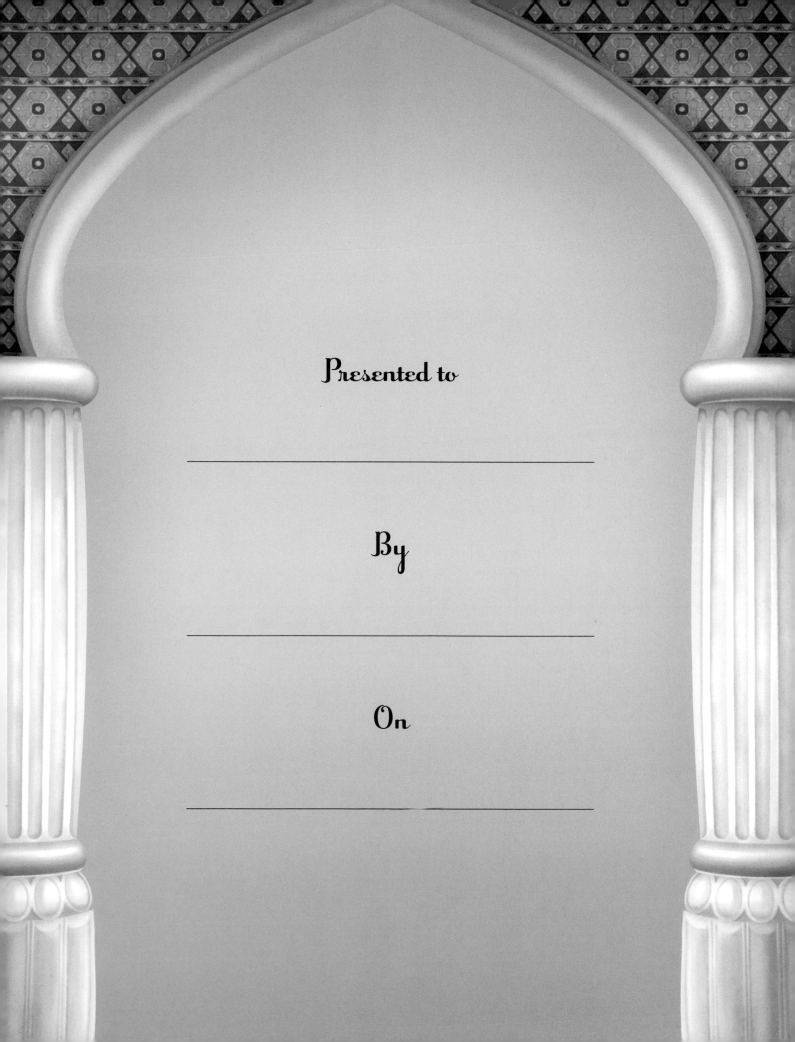

Presented to

_____

By

_____

On

_____

ZONDERKIDZ

Once Upon a Time Storybook Bible
Copyright © 2017 Zondervan
Illustrations © 2017 by Omar Aranda

Requests for information should be addressed to:

Zonderkidz, 3900 Sparks Drive SE, Grand Rapids, Michigan 49546

Art direction and design: Kris Nelson/StoryLook Design

Printed in China

17 18 19 20 21 /DSC / 21 20 19 18 17 16 15 14 13 12 11 10 9 8 7 6 5 4 3 2 1

Once Upon A Time

STORYBOOK BIBLE

Illustrated by Omar Aranda

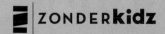

The Greatest Stories Ever Told

Welcome to your storybook Bible.

Inside these pages are some of the greatest stories ever told … and believe it or not they're real! All of these stories come from the Bible.

In this book you will meet vicious giants, hungry lions, and fish that can swallow people whole. You'll see awesome angels and amazing miracles. You'll read about heroes, villains, and the ultimate fight between good and evil. There are dozens of people, places, and wonders waiting to be discovered by *you*. So let's begin the way great stories often do with ***Once upon a time …***

Old Testament

New Testament

Old Testament

God Creates the World

"In the beginning, God created the heavens and the earth."
—GENESIS 1:1

Once Upon a Time ... God created the heavens and the earth. But the earth was blacker than black with darkness. And there was nothing but emptiness.

So God said, "Let there be light!"

God knew this light was very good, but he did not stop there. He looked upon earth and said, "Now, let there be sky."

God spun layer upon layer of fresh, clean air around the earth, wrapping it in every shade of blue.

Then God poured out waters all over the earth. He made them flow pure and clean and clear.

God divided this gigantic body of water by forming huge mountains and wide valleys, rolling hills, and smooth, flat plains.

Next, God made the earth's soil rich and good. "Let the land produce!" commanded God.

Plants of all kinds began to spring forth from the soil. Luscious green grasses grew, and fragrant flowers bloomed in every color. God painted the earth in breathtaking color and beauty. And it was so good!

God looked upon the sleeping seas and created new life to grow there. He made tiny sea creatures and funny squids. He made gigantic whales and powerful sharks! And to all these creatures God said, "Now grow and multiply and fill the sea."

"Let birds fill the skies," said God. And it was done. Bright-colored birds, in all sizes and shapes, swept across the sky. And each day they lifted their voices in joyful praise.

The earth was a wonderful place, a beautiful place, but God had even more ideas.

So he created all kinds of animals. He made tigers with stripes and elephants with floppy ears.

He made polar bears with warm, fuzzy coats, and penguins that could slide in the snow. He made bears and cougars. He made horses and cows, dogs and cats, pigs and goats.

And it was good.

Happily Ever After

What an amazing start to the story!
Out of nothing, God created an entire world.
Thank you, Lord,
for your incredible creation.

GENESIS 1:1–25

Adam and Eve in the Garden of Eden

"Your word is like a lamp that shows me the way.
It is like a light that guides me."

—PSALM 119:105

Once Upon a Time ... God looked at all he had made, and it was good. But it was still not enough. God wanted to create someone like himself. Someone who could be a friend. So God scooped up a handful of dust from the earth. Then he gently blew his life into it. And God made man. God named this man Adam and set him in a very special garden called Eden.

After a while, Adam became very lonely. God did not want Adam to be lonely, so he made him fall asleep. While Adam slept, God took out one of Adam's ribs and created a woman from it.

Adam was very pleased with his new friend. He named the woman Eve, and they lived very happily in their beautiful garden home. The only rule God gave them was they couldn't eat fruit from a tree in the middle of the garden. If they did, they would die.

One day a serpent spoke to Eve.

"Did God say you can't eat fruit from any of the trees in the garden?"

"No," explained Eve. "God said we could eat from all of the trees, except for the one in the middle."

"Surely you won't die if you try a bite," hissed the sly serpent.

So Eve plucked a piece from the tree and ate it. She shared the fruit with Adam.

When Adam told God what they had done, God was very sad. He cursed the serpent for tricking Eve, and he told Adam and Eve they had to leave the beautiful garden.

Happily Ever After

*Adam and Eve learned an important lesson:
God's rules are always right.
Do your best to follow God's rules every day.*

GENESIS 2–3

Noah Builds an Ark

"I have put my rainbow in the clouds.
it will be the sign of the covenant
between me and the earth."
—GENESIS 9:13

Once Upon a Time ... The years passed, and more and more people filled the earth. They no longer listened to God. Instead they spent every hour of every day thinking up ways to hurt and destroy, ways to cheat and steal.

God grew very sad. Finally, God said, "I will get rid of mankind entirely. In fact, I will remove all that moves and breathes from the face of the earth."

But before God wiped the entire earth clean, he thought about his good friend, Noah. Noah had always done what was right. So God told Noah to build an enormous ark. It would be bigger than anything that had ever been built before.

It took a long time, but finally Noah finished building the ark. Then God told Noah to load a male and female of each kind of animal onto the ark. God also told Noah to gather food for all the animals and for his family too. Enough for many days. Finally, the ark was loaded.

Then it began to rain. For forty long days it rained. Every living thing was wiped from the earth except for Noah and his family and the animals on the ark. They floated on the waters for more than one hundred and fifty days.

Finally, God began to dry the land. When Noah and his family and all the animals left the ark, they rejoiced and thanked God. And when they looked up, they saw that God had put a promise across the sky—a rainbow!

God said, "Never again will I destroy the earth with a flood."

Happily Ever After

Noah and his family had a scary adventure, but God kept them safe. If you trust in God, he will keep you safe too!

GENESIS 6–9

Joseph Goes to Egypt

"When you hope, be joyful. When you suffer, be patient.
When you pray, be faithful."

—ROMANS 12:12

Once Upon a Time ... A man named Jacob had twelve sons, but his youngest, Joseph, was his favorite. He made Joseph a beautiful coat with all the colors of the rainbow woven into it. This made Joseph's brothers jealous.

One night, Joseph had an unusual dream. The next day, he told his brothers, "I dreamed we were bundling up wheat. Suddenly, my bundle of wheat rose high in the air and all of your bundles bowed down before it."

"So you must think you're better than we are," scolded his brothers. "Shall we bow down to you now?" They were very angry.

One day, Jacob sent Joseph to check on his brothers who were tending sheep. When Joseph arrived, they jumped on him, ripped off his beautiful coat, and threw him down into a deep hole. When a band of merchants passed by, the brothers sold Joseph as a slave and he was taken to Egypt.

When Joseph was in Egypt, the king of the land, called Pharaoh, summoned him. He'd heard Joseph could explain dreams, and Pharaoh had had a dream he didn't understand.

God showed Joseph what the pharaoh's dream meant. Joseph said, "God is warning you. After seven years with plenty of food, the rains will stop. Nothing will grow for the next seven years. But if you plan, you can save your people from starvation."

"You are a wise man, Joseph," said Pharaoh. "You shall be in charge of all this."

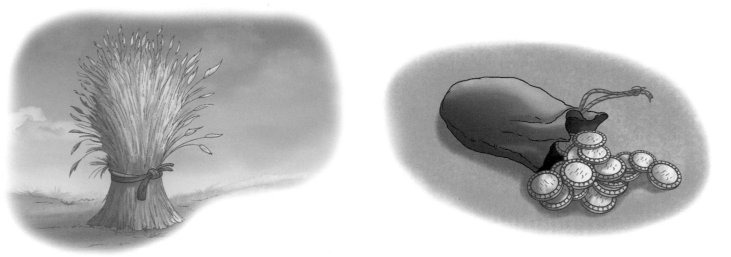

Joseph made sure that grain was stored. And when the bad years came, Egypt had plenty of food to feed its people.

During the famine, people from all over came to Egypt for food. Even Joseph's brothers came to buy grain.

Joseph invited the brothers into his home. But Joseph didn't say who he was until they were leaving. Then Joseph cried out, "I am Joseph! God spared me so I could help you." The brothers were reunited at last.

Happily Ever After

You may find yourself in a tough situation like Joseph did, but trust that God has a plan for you.

GENESIS 37–46

Baby Moses in the River

"I am with you.
I will watch over you everywhere you go."
—GENESIS 28:15

Once Upon a Time ... A new Egyptian pharaoh ruled in Egypt. The Israelites still lived in Egypt, but the pharaoh had made them slaves. The number of Israelites continued to grow, so the evil pharaoh ordered that all Israelite baby boys be thrown into the Nile River.

One mother could not bear to lose her beautiful baby boy. So she wove a sturdy basket in the shape of a tiny boat and made it watertight. Then she kissed her baby and set his basket afloat in the reeds along the Nile River.

Later that day, a princess was by the river and heard the baby's cries in the reeds. "Bring me that basket," she said to her handmaidens. The baby's sister, Miriam, waited nearby. "Poor little thing," said the princess.

"Shall I fetch someone to care for him?" asked Miriam. The princess agreed, and Miriam ran home and got her mother.

The baby boy was spared! And his very own mother took care of him.

"I shall name him Moses," said the princess, "for I took him up out of the water." And she raised him as her son.

Happily Ever After

What a miracle for Moses and his family. God was watching over him— just as he watches over you.

EXODUS 1–2

Moses Frees His People

"It is God's power to save everyone who believes."
—ROMANS 1:16

Once Upon a Time ... Moses grew up, and he left Egypt and became a shepherd. One day, as he tended sheep, he saw a bush that was on fire. But even though the flames leaped high, the bush didn't burn up.

"Moses! Moses!" called God. "I am the God of your people." Moses fell to his knees and hid his face in fear.

"I have seen my people suffering," said God. "I have come to deliver them out of Egypt and into a land that flows with milk and honey. And you, Moses, will go to Pharaoh. You will lead my people out of Egypt!"

Moses obeyed God. He gathered his family and returned to Egypt. God used Moses to perform fantastic miracles. But Pharaoh wouldn't listen to God.

So God sent nine terrible plagues to Egypt. He made rivers run with blood. He sent an army of frogs, swarms of gnats, and millions of flies. Animals died and Egyptians became covered in horrible, itching sores. Then God sent locusts, and hail, and three days of darkness.

Time after time, Pharaoh refused to let God's people go.

Finally, God sent one last plague. This time, all the firstborn sons of the Egyptians would be killed unless Pharaoh let the Israelites go. But he wouldn't.

God did as he said. Many Egyptians died, including Pharaoh's own son. But the Israelites were spared. At last, Pharaoh shouted, "GO!"

Moses led the people out of Egypt. Finally, Moses stopped at the banks of the Red Sea and waited for God. Meanwhile, back in Egypt, Pharaoh changed his mind. He gathered his army to capture the Israelites.

When the Israelites saw the army in the distance, they grew terrified. "Don't be afraid," said Moses. "Watch and see what God is able to do!" Moses reached out his hand over the Red Sea. God pushed aside the waters, and blew a mighty wind that divided the sea in half! The Israelites walked through the sea on dry ground. When Pharaoh's army tried to follow, God made the walls of water fall back into the sea!

As the Israelites watched Pharaoh's army being buried by the Red Sea, they knew their God was very powerful. They trusted him. And they trusted Moses.

Happily Ever After

God's power is incredible.
The next time you face a big problem,
trust in God and pray for his help.
You'll be amazed at what can happen!

EXODUS 2–15

The Battle of Jericho

"I am the Lord.
I am the God of all people.
Is anything too hard for me?"

—JEREMIAH 32:27

Once Upon a Time ... Moses grew old and a man named Joshua became leader of the Israelites. God said to Joshua, "Lead my people across the Jordan River. Each place you set your foot will be yours. I am with you wherever you go."

Soon Joshua reached a city called Jericho. There was a huge wall all around the city. It was tall and strong, and at first Joshua and his men didn't know how they could ever get past it.

God told Joshua exactly what to do in order to take the city of Jericho. So Joshua gathered men into an army to march around the city. Then came seven priests with ram's horn trumpets. They paraded around Jericho one time each day for six days. During this time, the priests blew on their trumpets.

On the seventh day, the Israelites paraded around Jericho six times. The priests blew their trumpets. On the seventh time around the city, Joshua called out a signal. Everyone yelled with all their might! And at that noise, the walls of Jericho fell.

Happily Ever After

Thanks to God, Joshua was able to do the impossible. Nothing, not even a huge wall made of stone, is too big for God to handle.

JOSHUA 1–6

Samson's Strength

"I can do all this by the power of Christ.
He gives me strength."
—PHILIPPIANS 4:13

Once Upon a Time ... As the years passed, the people of Israel forgot to obey God. Soon they were captured by the Philistines, a people who hated God.

One day, an angel appeared to an Israelite woman telling her she would have a son who would save Israel from the Philistines.

When the woman's son was born, she named him Samson. He grew up to be the strongest man ever!

For years, Samson battled the Philistines. One time, he fought an army and when the fight ended, Samson killed 1,000 Philistines with the jawbone of a donkey!

Samson loved a woman named Delilah, who really worked for the Philistines.

"Why are you so strong, Samson?" she asked. And although she begged, Samson wouldn't tell.

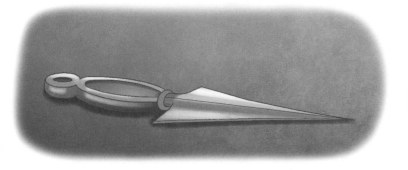

Finally, she cried, "You don't love me, Samson, or you would share your secret."

"If my hair is cut, my strength will go," Samson whispered.

That night when Samson fell asleep, the Philistines cut his hair. Samson's strength was gone.

The Philistines bound and blinded him and took him to their temple. But Samson prayed. And God gave him strength to push and collapse their temple.

Happily Ever After

Samson's great strength came from God. The next time you need to be strong, pray to God for him to make you as tough as Samson.

JUDGES 13–16

Ruth and Naomi

"In everything, do to others what
you would want them to do to you."

—MATTHEW 7:12

Once Upon a Time ... A woman
named Naomi lived far from her homeland.
Her husband and sons had died. All she had
left were her two daughters-in-law. One day,
Naomi told them, "I am returning to my
homeland."

"Please, Naomi," begged Ruth, one of the
daughters-in-law. "Let me go where you go.
Your people will be my people. And your God
will be my God."

So the two women traveled to Bethlehem.

"It's time for the barley harvest, Naomi," said Ruth. "If I gather leftover grain, we can make bread to eat." So Ruth picked up grain missed by the harvesters.

A man named Boaz owned the field and wondered who she was. "She came back with old Naomi," said his foreman. "All day long she has worked hard."

Boaz called Ruth and said, "Gather as much grain as you need, and my workers will watch for you. You helped my relative Naomi. May God bless you."

One night, Naomi told Ruth to go to the place where Boaz was sleeping. She told Ruth to wait for him there.

"What are you doing here?" Boaz asked when he woke up.

"Naomi has sent me," said Ruth. "Since you are her nearest relative, I have come to ask you to care for us."

"I will take care of you," said Boaz.

Naomi rejoiced. Ruth and Boaz were married, and Ruth became the great-grandmother of King David!

Happily Ever After

Ruth was a good daughter-in-law to Naomi, and a good friend. Think about how you can be a friend to the people in your life.

RUTH 1–4

Hannah's Prayer

"I will not break my covenant.
I will not go back on my word."

—PSALM 89:34

Once Upon a Time ... There lived a woman named Hannah. Hannah loved God. But she was sad, for she had no children. Each year, her husband took her to a place called Shiloh, and Hannah prayed a special prayer that God would give her a child.

One year, she prayed, "Dear God, if you will only give me a son, I will give him back to you, to serve you all his days."

The following year, Hannah's prayers were answered. She had a baby boy named Samuel!

She cared for Samuel until he was old enough to leave her. Then she kept her promise to God and took Samuel to live with the priests in Shiloh.

God gave Hannah many more children. And Hannah was pleased to know that Samuel was growing up in Shiloh, where he would love and serve God always.

Happily Ever After

God gave Hannah a great gift,
and she kept her promise to him.
God loves when we keep our promises.
He always keeps his.

1 SAMUEL 1

Samuel Listens to God

"Whoever belongs to God hears what God says."
—JOHN 8:47

Once Upon a Time ... Young Samuel was lying in bed when he heard a voice calling. He thought it was the old priest Eli, but Eli said, "I didn't call you; go back and lie down."

Samuel heard the call again, but Eli still said it wasn't him.

When Samuel heard it a third time, Eli said, "It must be God. Go back and listen." So Samuel went back, and God spoke.

But Samuel didn't want to tell Eli what God had said, because God was very unhappy with Eli's sons.

"Do not hide God's words from me," said Eli. And so Samuel told Eli. From then on Samuel always said what God told him to say.

Samuel continued to serve God as he grew older. The Israelites knew Samuel was a man they could trust to speak God's words. People all over Israel respected Samuel. And for a while, they lived in peace. Samuel helped them to remember to listen to God.

Happily Ever After

Listening to God is very important. You may not always hear his voice with your ears, but he is always speaking in your heart.

1 SAMUEL 3, 8

David and Goliath

"So do not be afraid. I am with you …
I will make you strong and help you.
I will hold you safe in my hands."

—ISAIAH 41:10

Once Upon a Time … A boy named David was delivering food to his brothers who were battling an army of Philistines. He heard a Philistine giant shouting at the Israelite army and making fun of them. The giant was tall and strong and carried many weapons.

"Who is that man?" asked David. His brothers told him about Goliath the mighty warrior. But David wasn't afraid of the giant. When the king heard of David's bravery, he called David before him.

"Don't worry, I'll go fight that giant," said David.

"But he's a warrior," said the king. "You're only a boy."

"God will help me kill this giant," said David.

The king gave David his armor and weapons. But they were too big for David.

So without any armor, David faced the giant. He stopped by a stream to pick up some stones. Then he stood before Goliath.

David looked up and said, "You come against me with weapons, but I come against you in the name of the Lord Almighty." Then David put a stone in his sling and swung it around until the sling whistled. The stone whizzed through the air and smacked Goliath right in the forehead. And the giant fell to the ground.

Happily Ever After

Even if you have to face a giant like Goliath, you never need to be afraid. God is always on your side, just like he was with David.

1 SAMUEL 17

David Becomes King

"The LORD is my shepherd.
He gives me everything I need."
—PSALM 23:1, A PSALM OF DAVID

Once Upon a Time ... When David grew older, he became the new king of Israel. David led the Israelites through many victorious battles against their enemies. Before long, David conquered Jerusalem and it was then called the City of David. He built a palace there.

With all their enemies defeated, Israel enjoyed a time of peace. David loved God, and his greatest wish was to build a temple for God. But David didn't always obey God. So finally God told David that David's son would be the one to build God his temple.

While David was king, he wrote many beautiful songs. Most were to praise God, but some were to say he was sorry. David loved to worship God with his songs.

Happily Ever After

It is important to worship God, whether that's with your words, your thoughts, or your actions. David knew this, which is why he wrote songs. You can read many of those songs in the Bible in the book of Psalms.

2 SAMUEL 1–7

Wise King Solomon

"If any of you needs wisdom,
you should ask God for it. He will give it to you.
God gives freely to everyone and doesn't find fault."

—JAMES 1:5

Once Upon a Time . . . After King David died, his son, Solomon, became Israel's king.

One night, God appeared to King Solomon in a dream. "Ask for whatever you want," said God.

"You did so much for my father," said Solomon. "But now I am king and I don't know how to rule. So please make my heart wise so that I can do what is right for your people."

God was glad that Solomon didn't ask for riches or long life. God granted King Solomon's wish, and Solomon became the wisest man ever. God also gave Solomon a long life and great riches.

Then, just as God had promised David, Solomon built God's temple. It took seven years to complete the beautiful building. Skilled craftsman decorated it with carved wood and fine gold.

When it was finished, Solomon held a huge celebration. For fourteen days the people worshiped God at the temple.

Although the temple was wonderful, Solomon knew that it was not great enough to contain the Almighty God. But God promised Solomon that his eyes and heart would always be on the temple and with his people.

Happily Ever After

Solomon knew it was better to have
wisdom than all the money in the world.
If you ask him,
God will make you wise too.

1 KINGS 3–9

Queen Esther's Bravery

"When I called out to you, you answered me.
You made me strong and brave."

—PSALM 138:3

Once Upon a Time . . . King Xerxes ruled Persia. When he needed a wife, his servants searched the land for the most beautiful women. A lovely woman named Esther was chosen. She was good and wise. But she was an Israelite. Her relative, Mordecai, warned her not to tell anyone she was an Israelite.

When King Xerxes met Esther, he was very pleased. He set the royal crown on her head, and she became his wife and queen.

Later, a powerful man named Haman became angry with Mordecai. Haman knew that Mordecai was an Israelite, and he encouraged King Xerxes to make it legal to kill Israelites.

Esther knew this law meant she too could die. "I will do all I can to change this," she said to Mordecai. "Please ask my people to pray for me."

And Mordecai did.

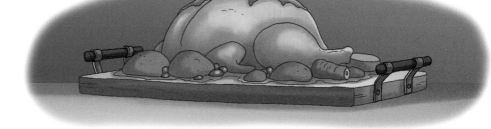

Esther invited the king and Haman to two nights of feasting. Then she asked for the king's mercy.

"Dear King," said Esther. "If you are pleased with me, I beg you to spare my life. And also spare the lives of my people. Don't put us to death."

"Who dares to do this?" demanded the king.

"It is this cruel Haman," said Esther, pointing to her enemy.

The king ordered Haman to be taken away. Esther and her people were safe.

Happily Ever After

Esther was brave to face Haman and the king. God gave her the courage she needed to save her people. He makes all of us brave when we need to be.

ESTHER 1–8

The Fiery Furnace

"The LORD is our God.
The LORD is the one and only God."
—DEUTERONOMY 6:4

Once Upon a Time ... Israel had been defeated by people called the Babylonians and taken captive.

The king of Babylon ordered his workers to build a giant golden statue. The king made a law commanding everyone to bow down and worship the statue whenever they heard the king's special music.

But Shadrach, Meshach, and Abednego were Israelites. They refused to worship the statue. They would only worship the one true God. So the king ordered the men be thrown into a fiery furnace. But first he said, "Make the fire seven times hotter than usual!"

The king watched as they were thrown into the furnace. He noticed something strange happening.

"Weren't only three men thrown into the fire?" asked the king. "I see four men," he said, "and one of them looks like a god!"

The king approached the furnace. "Shadrach, Meshach, Abednego!" he yelled. "Servants of the Most High God, come out!"

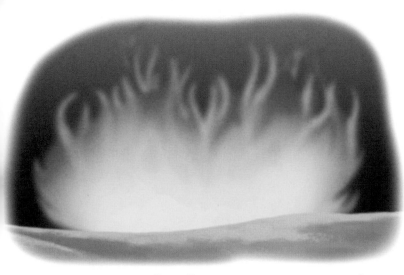

So the three came out. Nothing on them was burnt, and they didn't even smell of smoke.

"Your God is great!" cried the king. "He sent his angel to rescue you. From now on, no one will be allowed to say anything bad about your God."

Happily Ever After

The king of Babylon learned that there is only one true God. Shadrach, Meshach, and Abednego knew better—they wouldn't bow to the statue. They would only bow to God.

DANIEL 3

Daniel and the Lions

"The LORD will keep you from every kind of harm.
He will watch over your life."
—PSALM 121:7

Once Upon a Time ... King Darius ruled Babylon. King Darius respected Daniel, an Israelite advisor. He knew Daniel was a godly man who had served the kings before him. But some of King Darius' men did not like Daniel. They wanted to get rid of him. So they convinced the king to make a law forbidding people to pray to anyone but the king. Anyone who broke this law would be thrown into the lions' den.

Daniel knew about the law, but he continued to pray to God. The men spied on Daniel and told the king that Daniel had broken the law.

The king sadly agreed, and Daniel was put into the lions' den.

"May your God rescue you," said the king.

That night, the king could not eat or sleep. He was too worried about Daniel.

Early the next morning, he ran out to the lions' den.

"Daniel!" he cried. "Has your God been able to rescue you from the hungry lions?"

"King Darius," called Daniel, "my God sent his angel to shut the lions' mouths! They have not hurt me."

Daniel had been saved!

Happily Ever After

See what the power of God can do?
He kept Daniel safe from a den of hungry lions.
Say thank you to God for his
amazing power and protection.

DANIEL 6

Jonah and the Big Fish

"Trust in the Lord with all your heart.
Do not depend on your own understanding.
In all your ways obey him. Then he will make
your paths smooth and straight."

—PROVERBS 3:5–6

Once Upon a Time ... God spoke to a man named Jonah. "Jonah," said God, "go to Nineveh and tell the people I've seen their wickedness."

But Jonah didn't like the people of Nineveh. He thought he could run away from God. So he got on a ship sailing away from Nineveh.

Soon a storm came. The wind roared and the waves crashed around the ship. Jonah realized he was the reason for the terrible storm.

"Throw me overboard," said Jonah, "and the storm will end."

The sailors didn't want to throw Jonah out, but they agreed. They threw Jonah into the sea. Instantly, the sea became calm.

Then God sent a gigantic fish to swallow Jonah. For three days and three nights, Jonah stayed inside the fish. While he was in the fish, he asked God to help him.

Finally, God made the fish spit Jonah out onto dry land. This time, Jonah went straight to Nineveh and began to preach.

The people listened to Jonah. They were sorry for the bad things they had done. They began to pray. The people of Nineveh returned to God.

Happily Ever After

God wants us to do the right thing.
Even if we get off track or run away like
Jonah did, God will help us find our
way to where we're meant to be.

JONAH 1–3

New Testament

Mary and the Angel

"'I know the plans I have for you,' announces the LORD.
'I want you to enjoy success.
I do not plan to harm you.
I will give you hope for the years to come.'"
—JEREMIAH 29:11

Once Upon a Time ... An angel appeared to a young woman named Mary. "God is happy with you," said the angel. "You have been chosen to have a special baby boy. You will call him Jesus, and he will be great. He will be the Son of the Most High!"

Mary stared at the angel. "How can this be?" she asked.

"Don't worry, Mary. The Holy Spirit will come to you," said the angel. "Nothing is impossible with God."

Mary bowed. "I am God's humble servant. I will do all that you have said." Then the angel left.

Mary was engaged to marry a man named Joseph.

Joseph did not understand why Mary was chosen to have this baby.

Then one night, an angel appeared to Joseph in a dream. The angel said, "Joseph, do not be afraid to take Mary as your wife. For God has chosen her to give birth to his very own Son. This child shall be called Jesus, and he will save all people from sin."

Happily Ever After

Mary and Joseph were given a very important job. They were going to be the parents of Jesus! Sometimes God gives us big jobs, but he will always be there to help us.

LUKE 1

Jesus Is Born

"Jesus said, 'Let the little children come to me.
Don't keep them away. The kingdom of heaven
belongs to people like them.'"
—MATTHEW 19:14

Once Upon a Time ... A law was passed
that everyone must travel to their hometown to be
counted. Although Mary was almost ready to have
her baby, she and her husband Joseph had to go to
Bethlehem.

After a long, tiring journey, they reached the small
town. Mary knew it was time for God's Son to be
born. She was very tired from traveling and needed a
place to rest.

Many people crowded the streets of Bethlehem—
they too had come to be counted. And although
Joseph searched the whole town, he could not find a
room for them to stay in.

At last, Joseph found a shelter for Mary to rest. It was only a stable for oxen, cattle, and donkeys, but it was exactly right—the very place God had chosen.

Before long, Mary gave birth to God's only Son. Mary wrapped sweet baby Jesus in clean strips of soft cloth. Then she gently laid him on the straw in a manger.

Happily Ever After

*Jesus began his life as a little baby—
just like you did! So any time you feel too
young or too small, ask Jesus for guidance.
He knows exactly how you feel.*

LUKE 2

A Visit from the Wise Men

"Jesus answered, 'I am the way and the truth and the life.
No one comes to the Father except through me.
If you really know me, you will know my
Father also. From now on, you do know him.
And you have seen him.'"

—JOHN 14:6–7

Once Upon a Time ... After Jesus was born, wise men journeyed to Jerusalem. They had learned that a King had been born in that region. They stopped at King Herod's palace.

"Where is this newborn King?" asked the wise men. "We have seen his star and know that he is to be King of the Jews. We want to worship him."

But King Herod did not want to share his throne with anyone.

King Herod called in priests and scribes. "What do the prophets say about a King like this?" he demanded.

"The prophets say a very special King will be born in the town of Bethlehem," explained the men. "And he will be a shepherd to God's people."

King Herod went back to the wise men and told them to seek this King in Bethlehem. "And when you find him," said King Herod, "you must return and tell me where he is, so I can worship him too." But the truth was, King Herod did not wish to worship Jesus—he wanted to get rid of him.

The wise men traveled to Bethlehem and found Mary, Joseph, and baby Jesus. They worshiped Jesus and presented him with valuable gifts of gold, frankincense, and myrrh.

Later, an angel came and warned the wise men not to return to Herod's palace to tell the evil king about baby Jesus. He also warned Joseph to flee from Bethlehem.

And so Joseph quickly took Mary and Jesus to Egypt, where they stayed until it was safe to return.

Happily Ever After

The wise men knew how important Jesus was.
That's why they worshiped him.
You can worship Jesus too.

MATTHEW 2

Jesus Is Baptized

"There are different kinds of gifts. But they are all given to believers by the same Spirit. There are different ways to serve. But they all come from the same Lord."

—1 CORINTHIANS 12:4–5

Once Upon a Time ... Many years after the birth of Jesus, a man named John the Baptist began to preach around Judea. He wore a garment made of camel's hair and ate grasshoppers and wild honey. "Repent," he cried. "And stop doing wrong! God's Kingdom is coming soon!" People from miles around came to hear John preach. And hundreds prayed, telling God they were sorry for their sins. Then John baptized them in the Jordan River.

"I will baptize with water," John explained to the crowds. "But a greater One is coming! He will baptize you with the Holy Spirit—and with fire!"

Jesus traveled to the place where John was preaching. He asked John to baptize him. "I, baptize you?" cried John. "I am not fit to carry your sandals. You should baptize me!"

"Please," said Jesus. "It is right for you to do so." And so John obeyed Jesus.

As Jesus rose from the water, the heavens split open and God's Spirit landed upon Jesus in the form of a beautiful dove. A voice spoke from heaven, "This is my beloved Son, and I am very pleased with him!"

Happily Ever After

John was afraid he wasn't important enough to help Jesus. But Jesus wants all of us to use our special gifts to help him. Ask Jesus what you can do for him today.

MATTHEW 3

A Mountaintop Teaching

"Never stop praying."
—1 THESSALONIANS 5:17

Once Upon a Time … Jesus took his special followers, called disciples, to a quiet mountainside. "You are the light of the world!" he said to them. "When you light a lamp, do you put a bucket on top of it? No, of course not! You set it on a table so the whole house is lit by it. Let your life shine like a bright light so others will see and praise God the Father for the good he is doing in you!"

Jesus then told them, "Be careful when you help people or give to those in need. Make sure you do it quietly and from your heart. Don't make a big show so people will praise you. And when you pray, don't use fancy words and talk loudly. But pray in a quiet place."

Jesus taught them this prayer:

Dear Father in heaven,

Your name is the most holy.

Let your kingdom rule,

Let your will be done,

On earth just like in heaven.

Give us what we need for today.

Forgive us when we do wrong,

And help us to forgive others who do wrong.

Lead us far away from what tempts us,

And save us from evil.

Your kingdom and power and glory

will last forever!

Amen.

Happily Ever After

God loves to hear your voice.
Pray the Lord's Prayer
and say thank you for the day.

MATTHEW 5–6

Feeding the Crowds

"You are the God who does miracles.
You show your power among the nations."

—PSALM 77:14

Once Upon a Time … Jesus wished to get away from the busy towns, so Jesus and his disciples took a boat across the Sea of Galilee. But as they sailed, they spotted a huge crowd walking along the shore. When the boat reached the other side, Jesus went up on a mountainside and sat down with his disciples. When Jesus looked up he saw the crowd coming toward them. He turned to his disciple Philip and asked, "Where shall we buy food for these people?"

Philip looked up in surprise. "It would take a fortune to feed all these people!"

"Here's a boy who's willing to share," announced one of the disciples. "He has five loaves of bread and two little fish. That won't feed many people."

"Tell everyone to sit down," said Jesus. Soon the huge crowd was seated on the green, grassy slope.

Jesus thanked God for the boy's lunch. Then he broke the bread and fish and gave it to the disciples to pass out to the crowd. Everyone ate.

"Now," said Jesus, "gather all the leftovers, and be sure not to waste any." The disciples filled twelve baskets of leftovers. The crowd was amazed!

Happily Ever After

Jesus took something small—just a little bit of bread and fish—and turned it into something huge—a meal for 5,000 people! Tell Jesus thank you for the wonderful miracles he can do.

JOHN 6

He Walks on Water

"My eyes have seen your salvation."
—LUKE 2:30

Once Upon a Time ... Jesus needed time with his Father. So he went to the hills to pray.

As the sun set, the disciples began to sail across the lake. But when it became dark, the wind began to stir the waves, tossing the small boat back and forth. Then in the middle of the night, the disciples noticed something strange. A man was walking toward them, right on top of the water.

"It's a ghost!" they cried in terror.

"Don't be afraid!" called Jesus. "It is I."

Peter yelled, "If it's you, Lord, call me out to you!" Jesus called, and Peter climbed out of the boat. He began to walk on the water. But when his eyes looked away from Jesus and down at the frothing sea, Peter began to sink.

"Help me, Lord!" he cried. Jesus grabbed Peter's hand.

"Peter, where's your faith?" asked Jesus as they climbed into the boat.

But Peter and the other disciples could only bow down before Jesus.

"You really are the Son of God!" they said.

Happily Ever After

When Peter looked away from Jesus, he started to sink. But if you keep your eyes on Jesus, if you believe in him and follow his Word, you will always stay afloat.

MATTHEW 14

The Blind Man

"So I tell you, when you pray for something,
believe that you have already received it.
Then it will be yours."

—MARK 11:24

Once Upon a Time ... A crowd followed as Jesus approached the city of Jericho. At the edge of town sat a poor blind man named Bartimaeus. When he heard that Jesus was passing by, he began to yell with all his might. "Jesus!" he cried. "Son of David, have mercy on me!" People nearby tried to quiet Bartimaeus. But the more they tried, the louder he shouted. "Son of David!" he hollered. "Please, have mercy on me!"

Jesus stopped walking and turned to his disciples. "Bring that man to me," he said.

The disciples went to Bartimaeus. "Get up!" they said. "Get on your feet and come with us. Jesus is calling for you."

Tossing down his cloak, the blind man went with them.

"What do you want me to do?" asked Jesus.

"Teacher," said Bartimaeus, "I wish to see."

"Go," said Jesus. "Because of your faith, you are healed."

Instantly, Bartimaeus could see. He followed Jesus, looking at everything as he went!

Happily Ever After

*Jesus helped Bartimaeus see again
because Bartimaeus had faith.
What do you need help with in your life?
Say a prayer to God and have faith.*

MARK 10

Zacchaeus the Tax Collector

"God is faithful and fair. If we confess our sins,
he will forgive our sins. He will forgive every wrong
thing we have done. He will make us pure."

—1 JOHN 1:9

Once Upon a Time ... Zacchaeus
was a tax collector who took money from
others. When Zacchaeus heard Jesus was in
town, he wanted to see him. But Zacchaeus
was short, and Jesus was always surrounded
by a crowd. So Zacchaeus decided to climb
a sycamore tree. From there he could watch
for Jesus.

Zacchaeus watched as Jesus stopped right beneath his tree. Jesus looked straight up at him.

"Zacchaeus," said Jesus with a smile. "Come on down. I want to stay at your house today."

Zacchaeus hopped down. "You are welcome at my house, Jesus," said the little man.

But others grumbled. "Why does Jesus want to stay with him? He's a sinner."

Zacchaeus turned to Jesus and said, "Look, Lord. I promise to give half of my money to the poor. If I have cheated anyone in taxes, I will pay them back four times that amount."

"Salvation comes to Zacchaeus's house today," announced Jesus. "I have come to look for and save those who are lost."

Happily Ever After

Zacchaeus wasn't always a good person, but Jesus wanted to be friends with him anyway. Jesus loves us no matter what mistakes we make.

LUKE 19

Lazarus, Wake Up!

"With God, all things are possible."
—MATTHEW 19:26

Once Upon a Time ... Jesus received a message from his friends Mary and Martha, saying their brother Lazarus was sick.

After two days, Jesus said he would go to see Lazarus.

Martha met Jesus at the edge of town. "Lord," she cried, "if you had been here sooner, my brother would be alive. Still, I know God will give you what you ask."

"Lazarus will come back to life," said Jesus. "I am the resurrection and the life. Anyone who believes in me will live even if he dies. Do you believe in this, Martha?"

"Yes, Lord," she answered.

Martha went home to tell Mary that Jesus had come. Then Mary hurried to the edge of town too. "Lord," sobbed Mary, "if you had been here, my brother would not have died!"

"Where have you laid Lazarus?" Jesus asked.

As they walked, Jesus cried too.

"Remove the stone," Jesus commanded when they arrived, his face wet with tears.

"But, Lord," said Martha, "Lazarus has been dead for days."

"Believe and see God's glory," said Jesus.

In a loud voice he called, "Lazarus, come out!"

Out stepped a man wrapped in cloth. Lazarus was alive!

Happily Ever After

There is nothing Jesus cannot do!
Remember in good times and in bad,
Jesus is always on your side.

JOHN 11

Jesus in Jerusalem

"I give you a new command. Love one another.
You must love one another,
just as I have loved you."

—JOHN 13:34

Once Upon a Time ... Jesus came to Jerusalem. As Jesus entered the city, people put their coats and garments across the road. Others spread palm branches they had cut from the nearby trees. A joyful parade followed Jesus as he rode through Jerusalem.

"Hosanna! Hosanna!" they cried. "Blessed is he who comes in the name of the Lord! Hosanna in the highest!"

Jesus wanted to share a special meal with his disciples. He wanted to show his disciples how much he loved them. Before the meal, Jesus wrapped a towel around his waist and poured water into a bowl. Jesus washed all the disciples' feet, then he sat back down.

"See how I served you?" he asked. "I want you to serve each other in the same way. And if you do these things, you will be blessed."

Jesus ate supper with the disciples. As they ate, Jesus held up a piece of bread. First he gave thanks for it, then he broke it into pieces and shared it with his disciples.

"Take and eat this," he said. "This is my body."

Then Jesus took a cup of wine and gave thanks. He shared it with his disciples saying, "Drink from this cup. This is my blood which will be poured out so that many can receive forgiveness for their sins. Love each other the way I have loved you," said Jesus. "When people see how much you love each other, they will know you are my disciples."

Happily Ever After

Jesus showed his disciples how to care for one another. Think about ways you can show your friends and family you care about them.

MATTHEW 26, MARK 11, JOHN 13

The Darkest Day

"God so loved the world that he gave his one
and only Son. Anyone who believes in him
will not die but will have eternal life."

—JOHN 3:16

Once Upon a Time ... That night, Jesus
took his disciples to a quiet garden called Gethsemane
to pray. "Stay here and pray while I go over there,"
said Jesus. He knew it would soon be time to leave
the world and join God in heaven.

Jesus went ahead of them. He cried out to the
Father, "If it is possible, please remove this task from
me. But don't do my will, Father; only let your will be
done."

When Jesus returned to his disciples, he found
they had all fallen asleep. So, in his darkest hour,
Jesus prayed alone.

Men armed with swords and clubs marched to where Jesus and
the disciples stood. The guards seized Jesus. Then they took Jesus
to the home of the high priest to be questioned. The frightened
disciples ran away.

Jesus was sentenced to death. The soldiers placed a crown of
thorns on Jesus' head and led him to a place of death called The
Skull. They nailed his hands and feet to a rough wooden cross.

From the cross, Jesus looked down on the people and said,
"Forgive them, Father, for they don't know what they are doing."

Then, although it was still the middle of the day, darkness swallowed the sunlight. The air became still.

"Father!" cried Jesus. "Into your hands I commit my spirit!" Then Jesus breathed his last breath. And in that black and lonely moment, Jesus died.

The earth grew deathly silent. The sky remained dark. And down in Jerusalem, the great curtain in the temple was ripped from top to bottom!

"Surely this was a righteous man," said a centurion. Those who loved Jesus stood off in the distance crying.

Happily Ever After

Jesus gave his life to save the world.
He died so that one day,
you could join him in heaven.
Tell him thank you for his sacrifice.

MATTHEW 26, MARK 14, LUKE 22–23

He Lives!

"Trust in the Lord with all your heart."
—PROVERBS 3:5

Once Upon a Time ... Jesus was
buried, and a large stone was placed in front
of the opening to his tomb. Guards were
placed at the tomb to make sure no one
would steal Jesus' body.

After the Sabbath, Mary Magdalene went
to the tomb early in the morning. When she
reached the tomb, she found the stone was
rolled away.

She turned and ran back down the road until she came to two of Jesus' disciples.

"They have taken our Lord out of the tomb!" she cried. "I don't know where they have put him!"

The disciples ran on to the tomb too. They didn't know what to think. So the disciples returned to their homes.

Mary remained at the tomb, crying. But when she looked up, she saw two angels.

"Why are you crying, Mary?" asked the angels.

"They took my Lord," she said. "I don't know where they have put him."

Then Mary saw a man. She didn't recognize him. "Sir," she asked, "if you have taken him away, please tell me."

"Mary," he said. And instantly, Mary realized it was Jesus standing right in front of her.

"Teacher!" she cried.

"Go and tell the others," Jesus said. So Mary ran and told the others that Jesus had risen from the dead!

Happily Ever After

Jesus came back,
just like he said he would!
You can always trust in Jesus.

MATTHEW 27–28, JOHN 20

Jesus' Mission for You

"Tell the nations about his glory.
Tell all people about the wonderful things he has done."

—PSALM 96:3

Once Upon a Time ... Jesus told his disciples to meet him on a mountain, and there he gave them a special job to do.

"Go into the world," said Jesus, "and tell everyone the good news. Teach others how to be my disciples. Show them how to do the things I have taught you. And baptize them in the name of the Father and the Son and the Holy Spirit. And remember this: I will always be with you, even to the very end of time."

Many days later, the disciples were gathered in one place. Suddenly a sound like a loud, roaring wind whipped through the room. The disciples stared in wonder as a small flame came to rest on each one of them. In that same moment, they were all filled with the Holy Spirit. The power they received from the Holy Spirit made them able to speak in languages they had never known before.

The disciples went out into the streets, speaking their new languages. They told people how Jesus had died and come back to life, and how they too could be saved. When people heard the disciples talking about God in their own languages, they were amazed.

Three thousand people listened to this message and were baptized that very day!

Happily Ever After

Jesus wants you to share his message with the world. Think about ways you can tell others about Jesus.

MATTHEW 28, MARK 16, ACTS 2

Jesus Is Coming Back

"Christ is your life. When he appears again,
you also will appear with him in heaven's glory."

—COLOSSIANS 3:4

Once Upon a Time ... One of Jesus'
disciples, John, spent some time on an island.
While John was there, God showed him what it
will be like when Jesus takes his believers home
to heaven.

There will be a new heaven and a new earth.
All sadness, crying, sickness, and death will be
gone. The new city of God will be enormous
and beautiful.

A spectacular wall will surround the city like a glittering rainbow made of millions of colorful jewels. And there will be twelve giant gates in the wall, each made of solid pearl. The streets will be polished gold that glistens like glass. And the buildings will be a shimmering gold and glass.

There will be no need for the sun or moon, for God's glory will be brighter than the summer sun. A crystal-clear river of life will flow from the throne of God and through the city. The tree of life will grow there, bringing forth new fruit. And the leaves of this tree will heal all the nations.

Jesus said, "Behold, I am coming soon! I am the First and the Last, the Beginning and the End. Yes, I am coming soon."

Amen. Come, Lord Jesus.

Happily Ever After

One day, Jesus will return to the world to bring believers to that beautiful city. And he will be so excited to see you!

REVELATION 21–22

The End, and a Beginning

This book is at an end, but it is only the beginning of the story. Find many incredible stories just like these in your Bible, where you can learn more about everything from the creation of the world to Jesus' wonderful promise to return.

The End